The Buddha & Christ as Religious Teachers

Lily de Silva

BUDDHIST PUBLICATION SOCIETY
KANDY SRI LANKA

Published in 1992

Buddhist Publication Society
P.O. Box 61
54, Sangharaja Mawatha
Kandy, Sri Lanka

ISBN 955-24-0097-X

Typeset at the BPS
Text set in New Century Schoolbook

Printed in Sri Lanka by
Karunaratne & Sons Ltd.
647, Kularatne Mawatha
Colombo 10

THE WHEEL PUBLICATION NO. 380

The Buddha and Christ as Religious Teachers

Two Spiritual Leaders

The Buddha and Jesus Christ are two great spiritual leaders who founded two important world religions. Though they are similar in certain respects, they differ greatly one from the other as founders of religion, in the same way that their doctrines differ from one another. This paper aims at making a brief comparative study of these two great personages in their role as religious teachers.

In order to obtain a clear idea of the Buddha's spiritual leadership it is relevant to inquire into the virtues of the Buddha as enumerated in a stereotype formula which recurs often in the Pali Canon.[1] The formula recounts nine epithets of the Buddha, and it is noteworthy that this group of nine virtues is never applied to other disciples, not even to those who have reached the final goal. The latter are generally known by only one of the epithets, namely, *arahant*.

The Buddha is so called because he is the enlightened one. He is awake while the rest of the world is asleep. He is called the worthy one (*arahaṁ*) because he is immaculately pure in word, deed and thought, and never does anything blameworthy even in secret. He is the fully enlightened and self-enlightened one (*sammāsambuddho*). He is endowed with supramundane knowledge and noble exemplary conduct (*vijjācaraṇasampanno*). He has trod the same path as that followed by Buddhas of bygone days and arrived at the same peace of Nibbāna (*sugato*). He has thoroughly understood the nature of man and the world (*lokavidū*). He is the supremely magnanimous disciplinarian (*anuttaro purisadammasārathi),* and the teacher par excellence of gods and men (*satthā devamanussānaṁ*). He is the awakened one who awakens others (*buddho*). He is the fortunate one (*bhagavā*) because he is the very embodiment of all that is noble and good.

In this traditional list of nine virtues what is important for our present purpose is to observe that the Buddha is never spoken of as a saviour. Buddhas never play the role of saviour, they are essentially teachers and guides.[2] When a Buddha attains enlightenment he only saves himself. By teaching the path to others he helps others save themselves. Worldly existence is like a fearful wilderness where human beings are lost. Buddhas are pioneers who forge a way out of this wilderness, and through compassion for beings who are similarly lost, they teach the way out. Therefore Buddhas are path-finders and path-expounders. They are essentially spiritual teachers.

In contrast, Jesus Christ is always spoken of as the saviour. In fact even his name Jesus means the one who saves his people from their sins (Mt.12.1). He represents God on earth, he is the son of God incarnate. He is called the exemplar not only because he led an exemplary life, but because he was the perfect example of the character of God.[3] He is a revealer or a prophet because he is the spokesman of God who proclaimed the divine message. He had the authority on earth to forgive the sins of humans, therefore he was the redeemer or the saviour (Mt.9.6). His personal experience, interpreted as his "work," changed the moral relations of God and humans,[4] and his work of salvation involved not just his birth, but his death, resurrection and ascension.[5]

Even though there is a vast corpus of research done on the Bible, it is very surprising for a Buddhist to learn that there is hardly any research done on Jesus Christ in his capacity as a religious teacher. But the Bible speaks of Jesus Christ over and over again as going from place to place teaching and preaching to the people.

Wisdom of the Buddha and Jesus Christ

The Buddha stood before man and declared truths which he himself found and realized through his own intuitive wisdom. He did not appeal to any supernatural power for inspiration, guidance, authority or knowledge. He discovered truths which were unheard of before in known human history.[6] His realization was so profound and perfect that he uses five different phrases to describe different aspects of this deep spiritual awakening: vision arose (*cakkhuṁ udapādi*), wisdom arose (*ñāṇaṁ udapādi*), insight arose (*paññā udapādi*), knowledge arose (*vijjā udapādi*), and illumination arose (*āloko udapādi*).

The content of his supracognitive attainments is also spelt out in lucid detail. Of the higher knowledges he had, the most important three were retrocognition or the knowledge of remembering past lives (*pubbenivāsānussatiñāṇa*), clairvoyance with the special ability of seeing the death and rebirth of beings according to the working of kamma (*dibbacakkhu* or *cutūpapātañāṇa*), and the knowledge of the destruction of mental defilements (*āsavakkhayañāṇa*). These three knowledges he shared with most of his disciples who reached final liberation under his guidance. Three other knowledges which the Buddha possessed, but which were shared by some arahants only, were the ability to perform miracles (*iddhividha*), the divine ear (*dibbasota*), and telepathy or thought reading (*cetopariyañāṇa*). These three are not essential for liberation.

The Buddha also had certain unique intellectual capacities not shared by any of his arahant disciples. He could read the spiritual propensities of other people and thereby prescribe meditation topics which were particularly suitable for them.

He also had four "absolute confidences" (*vesārajjāni*) on account of which he could fearlessly face any assembly of learned men.[7] He had the absolute confidence that no human or divine being can reasonably accuse him:

(1) of not being fully enlightened;
(2) of not being free of all mental defilements;
(3) of being mistaken in declaring as dangerous things that do not in fact constitute dangers;
(4) of preaching a doctrine which does not lead to its professed goal.

Endowed with these absolute confidences the Buddha claims supreme eminence and authority among gods and men, which no arahant could ever claim.

When we turn to the Bible there are references to the wisdom and authority of Jesus Christ. Crowds that flocked to him from all corners were amazed at his wisdom and authority (Mt.7.28-29). Some exclaimed: Where did this man get this wisdom and these miraculous powers? Isn't this the carpenter's son? (Mt.13.54). The Bible does not spell out the cognitive sapiential attainments of Jesus Christ, so we do not really know what kinds of knowledge he may have had. But it is clearly stated that he derives authority from God, the father in heaven. The Son of Man has authority on earth to forgive sins (Mt.9.6). There is no doubt that his followers were simply amazed at the wisdom and conviction with which he exhorted them. Such words of wisdom they were not accustomed to as nothing like this had ever been seen in Israel (Mt.9.33).

When we consider the supernormal abilities of Jesus

Christ with a background of Buddhist learning we have to conclude that Jesus Christ had a training in mental culture. The miracles which he performed come under *iddhividha*, which is the first of the supernormal knowledges (*abhiññā*). *Iddhis* or miracles can be performed only by one who has developed the mind up to the fourth meditative level (*jhāna*). There is also evidence that he had developed some measure of thought reading (*cetopariyañāṇa*), for he knew that one among his twelve immediate disciples was going to betray him (Mt.26.21). It is possible that he had a limited measure of clairvoyance (*dibbacakkhu*) with the ability to see into one's life beyond death, how the righteous reach a happy celestial life and the wicked reach a woeful state. He regarded these as eternal destinies whereas the Buddhist view is that they are temporary abodes in the ever-recurring process of transmigration (*saṁsāra*). He also had some premonitions, for he had predicted his tragic death (Mt.16.21) and Peter's denial (Mark 14.30). Premonitions, however, are not classified under any of the *abhiññās* and the only category under which they could be included is clairvoyance (*dibbacakkhu*). Thus a Buddhist would conclude that Jesus Christ had developed *iddhividha* to a high degree, and *cetopariyañāṇa* and *dibbacakkhu* to a limited extent.

Compassion of the Buddha and Jesus Christ

Karuṇā is the Pali word for compassion and it is defined as the sublime emotional quality which moves the heart of noble people when others are in distress.[8] The commentary on the *Suttanipāta* defines it as the desire of wanting to remove the bane and sorrow of one's fellow beings.[9] This compassion is invariably coupled with loving-kindness (*mettā*), which is defined as the desire to bring welfare and happiness to one's fellow beings.[10] The Buddha has a heart that is cooled by the waters of compassion, and he is looked upon as the very epitome of compassion. This positive emotion is regarded as the very fountain of all Buddha virtues.[11] Impelled by great compassion, the bodhisatta—as a future Buddha is called during his preparatory training—made a firm determination to rescue suffering beings from the quagmire of continued existence (*saṁsāra*). With this determination he gradually fulfilled the perfections (*pāramitā*) over a long period of time and attained full enlightenment by self-effort. Therefore compassion is the very source of enlightenment.[12] It is also said that the Buddha enters into a meditative absorption of great compassion every morning to survey the world to pick out beings who are worthy of his mercy and help.[13]

The Buddha admonished his disciples too to practise loving-kindness (*mettā*) and compassion (*karuṇā*) towards all beings. This has to be cultivated in such profound measure so that one does not entertain a thought of anger toward one's tormentors even if they were to saw one up limb by limb.[14] Such is the profundity and purity of these sublime emotions cultivated by the Buddha and his noble disciples.

The very first precept enjoined on all lay Buddhists, the injunction against killing even the meanest living thing, is a precept prompted by compassion. Through experience one knows that one does not like to be killed. Therefore, taking the cue from one's own experience, one should abstain from killing.[15] All beings treasure life and life has to be respected as sacred.

When we turn to the Bible we find ample testimony to the compassion of Jesus Christ. It is said: Jesus went through all the towns and villages, teaching in their synagogues, preaching the good news of the kingdom and healing every disease and sickness. When he saw the crowds he had compassion on them, because they were harassed and helpless, like sheep without a shepherd (Mt.9.35-36). He showed much compassion to wrong-doers, and on being asked why he eats with tax-collectors and sinners, he said: It is not the healthy who need a doctor, but the sick (Mt.9.12).

But what epitomizes his compassion is his earnest appeal on behalf of his tormentors at the crucifixion: "Father, forgive them, for they do not know what they are doing" (Luke 23.34). Words exuding such deep sympathy and compassion for one's own tormentors could not have been uttered at a time of inhuman torture and excruciating physical pain, if Jesus Christ had not cultivated the sublime positive emotions of *mettā* and *karuṇā* to the highest possible level. This is an excellent and admirable instance of the admonition of the Buddha's "simile of the saw" being put into practice.[16] Thus a Buddhist would conclude that this is indisputable evidence that Jesus had developed liberation of the mind through loving-kindness (*mettā-cetovimutti*).

Jesus admonished his followers too to cultivate compassion: "Love your enemies and pray for those who persecute you" (Mt.5.44). For, if you forgive men when they sin against you, your heavenly Father also will forgive you. But if you do not forgive men their sins, your Father will not forgive your sins (Mt.6.14). Appealing to personal experience Jesus exhorts his followers: "In everything, do to others what you would have them do to you, for this sums up the law and the prophets" (Mt.7.12).

Purpose, Scope and Function of the Teachings

The Buddha had a clear-cut idea of the purpose and scope of his teachings. Humanity has a problem, that is, the problem of the unsatisfactory nature of human existence. This is not confined to a mere life span of a hundred years; it is an ever-recurring phenomenon. The Buddha discovered a way out of this misery and this was the message he wanted to convey to humankind. The purpose of his teaching was to lead humans out of suffering. The Buddha did not preach all that he discovered during the period of preparation and experimentation. He selected what was essential and relevant for liberation and preached only that much, nothing more and nothing less. What he realized he compared to the leaves in a forest, but what he chose to teach is like a handful of leaves.[17] He never kept back as knowledge reserved for the teacher (*ācariyamuṭṭhi*) anything that was relevant for liberation.[18]

During the time of the Buddha there was much speculation regarding philosophical problems such as the duration and extent of the world. The Buddha was never interested in philosophical speculations. As a pragmatist he did not want to get involved in such never-ending speculation and he strictly kept such problems aside as unprofitable and irrelevant issues.[19] Thus he limited himself to the problem of suffering and the way out of suffering.

What the Buddha did teach is relevant to human experience (*sandiṭṭhiko*), of immediate benefit to people and of timeless value (*akāliko*), open to verification (*ehipassiko*), leading to the goal of peace and happiness (*opanayiko*), and it can be individually realized by the wise (*paccattaṁ veditabbo viññūhi*).[20]

The Buddha emphasized that practice according to precept is of prime value. Knowledge of the Dhamma is important in so far as it is a guide for the practice. He who studies the Dhamma but does not act accordingly is compared to the cowherd who looks after somebody else's cattle but does not enjoy the dairy products. Such a person is also compared to the spoon which does not know the taste of the soup, whereas the one who practises is like the tongue that enjoys every flavour.[21]

The intuitive truths propounded by Buddhism can be known only through strict self-discipline, regular meditation and cultivated wisdom. Ethical life is but the initial step, it has to be followed by meditation or mental culture. After a long discourse the Buddha would often point out to his disciples shady trees and say: "Here are shady trees, sit down and meditate in order to discipline and cultivate the mind. All that a compassionate teacher can do for his disciples has been done by me. Do not be negligent. Do not leave room for regret later on."[22]

In the Alagaddupama Sutta the Buddha admonishes his disciples to be cautious in the study of the Dhamma.[23] One has to be as shrewd and cautious as when catching a venomous snake. If one does not correctly grip a venomous snake by its neck it can turn round and bite. Similarly the Dhamma can be dangerous if the correct pragmatic approach and attitude are lacking. If one tries to intellectualize truths which have to be experientially comprehended there is the danger that one will get lost in the wilderness of philosophical speculation. The moral danger of glorifying oneself in debate and condemning others is also ever present.

The Buddha has emphasized that the Dhamma has only instrumental value: it is for the purpose of crossing over and not for the purpose of grasping as a theory. It is compared to a raft which is to be discarded once the task of crossing the floods is accomplished.[24]

When we turn to the Bible, the teaching of the kingdom of God stands out as the central message. The phrase "kingdom of God" is taken from the Old Testament and it may have been mistaken by the Jews to mean the establishment of a secular nationalistic kingdom free from unrighteous foreign domination and oppression.[25] But what Jesus meant may have been a moral and spiritual kingdom to be established in the heart of man, not in a distant ideal future, but in the actual present according to the rule of God. That is the meaning of the message that the kingdom of God is near at hand (Mark 1.15; Luke 10.8,11).

Once, when he was asked by the Pharisees when the kingdom of God would come, Jesus replied: "The kingdom of God does not come visibly, nor will people say, 'Here it is,' or 'There it is,' because the kingdom of God is within you" (Luke 17.20-21). This kingdom is not materialistic, for it is said: "The kingdom of God is not a matter of eating and drinking, but of righteousness, peace and joy in the Holy Spirit" (Rom. 14.17). Whatever Jesus preached and did is relevant for this central message and it can be taken as the purpose and scope of his teachings.

There are many references in the Bible where Jesus exhorts his followers to put into practice what they learn from him. He who practises according to the teachings is like a wise man who builds his house on a rock. A storm cannot shatter it. He who does not is like a foolish man who builds his house on sand, for when the storm comes and rains beat against it, it falls with a great crash (Mt. 7.24-27). Jesus says: "Not who says to me, 'Lord, Lord,' will enter the kingdom of heaven, but only he who does the will of my Father who is in heaven" (Mt. 7.21). One of his disciples admonishes thus: "This is the message we have heard from him and declare to you. God is light, in him there is no darkness at all. If we claim to have fellowship with him, yet walk in the darkness, we lie and do not live by the truth. But if we walk in the light as he is in the light, we have fellowship with one another, and the blood of Jesus, his son, purifies us from all sin" (1 John1.5-7).

Sending out Disciples

The Buddha inaugurated his missionary activities with just five disciples. Preaching to them over a number of days, he guided them in the practice of the noble middle path consisting of self-discipline, mental culture and wisdom, and they soon realized the same noble truths which the Buddha himself had realized by self-effort. Thus arahants, liberated ones, were born in the world. In this manner the community soon multiplied and when there were sixty of them, blemishless in character, mature in wisdom and fully liberated, the Buddha advised them to go out into the world singly to spread the message for the welfare and happiness of the masses.[26] The Buddha wished them to go in different directions, each one taking a separate road so that the message could reach as wide a circle as possible.

The spiritual qualifications which the disciples had acquired comprised their own individual realization. They had first-hand experiential knowledge of the Dhamma, and they were in a position to explain it to others convincingly, without depending on the teacher or any other supernatural being for information, explanation or authority.

Jesus Christ too sent out his disciples to spread the message among his people in Israel. He instructed his disciples: "Do not go among the Gentiles or enter any town of the Samaritans. Go rather to the lost sheep of Israel. As you go preach this message: 'The kingdom of heaven is near.' Heal the sick, raise the dead, cleanse those who have leprosy, drive out demons" (Mt.10.5-8). Thus he gave them authority to drive out evil spirits and to heal every disease and sickness (Mt.10.1). It is, however, not known how this authority was transferred; the only surmise is that the disciples themselves had unflinching faith in God and they too were given the gift to heal. The Bible also does not say anything regarding the spiritual attainments of these disciples who were sent to preach to the people.

The Teacher-Disciple Relationship

The Buddha founded a community of monks that was non-exclusive, supraracial, supranational and world-embracing, called the Sangha. Just as all rivers enter the ocean and lose their individual identities, all those who enter the Sangha lose their caste, racial and national identities and come to be called recluses who are sons of the Sakyan sage (*samaṇā Sakyaputtiyā*).[27] The Buddha stands in *loco parentis* to his disciples. He had great compassion for them and it is testified by the fact that he made it a point to regularly visit their living quarters to see for himself their living conditions, health problems and spiritual application. It was on such an occasion that he found over-zealous Soṇa Koḷivisa with blistered soles practising meditation by walking up and down. Immediately he explained to Soṇa the danger and futility of over-enthusiasm with the simile of the lute and convinced him of the benefits of a balanced approach.[28] On another occasion he discovered a monk with oozing sores all over his body. He boiled water and bathed the monk himself, and having thus made him comfortable, gave him a discourse which proved to be of great spiritual benefit to him.[29]

The Buddha set an ideal example to his disciples by the nobility and the simplicity of the life he led. He practised what he preached and preached what he practised (*yathāvadī tathākārī, yathākārī tathāvādī*).[30] His life was an open book and he invited his disciples to scrutinize his behaviour and see for themselves whether the claim made by him that he is free from all mental defilements is true or not.[31] He never promulgated rules for the monks which he himself did not conform to.

Though a great disciplinarian, the Buddha exercised great caution and patience in handling monks who were immature and sensitive. He refrained from prodding them with too frequent admonitions lest they lose even the faith with which they joined the Order.[32] He also knew when to be stern and firm. According to the Cātuma Sutta he chased away a group of monks for noisy behaviour with the intention of disciplining them.[33] Pothila was a learned monk who instructed others, but failed to win spiritual distinction himself. The Buddha started addressing him as "Empty Pothila" (Tuccha Pothila).[34] He took up the hint and went to a monastery of arahants where his pride of learning was humbled. He exerted himself diligently and became an arahant.

In the Abhayarājakumāra Sutta the Buddha illustrated his sternness at times with a simile.[35] If a baby puts a pebble in his mouth an elder would take it out by force, even if the process hurts him, because he has great love and compassion for the baby. Similarly the Buddha sometimes uses stern measures out of compassion for his disciples. In the Mahāsuññatā Sutta he explains that disciples should entertain an attitude of friendliness and not hostility when the teacher, out of compassion and sympathy, spurs them on with instructions, pointing out their faults over and over again.[36]

Devotion of a personal nature is very much discouraged by the Buddha as that can even be an impediment for spiritual progress. Once the Buddha chided Vakkali, who had great admiration for him, by saying: "What is the use of looking at this rotten body of mine? He who sees the Dhamma sees me."[37]

Thus a friendly caring attitude characterized by non-attachment was fostered within the Sangha and it was most conducive to the spiritual progress of individual members.

According to the Bible the basis of the relationship between teacher and pupil is love and faith. It is said: "Love the Lord, your God with all your heart and with all your soul and with all your mind. This is the first and greatest commandment. And the second is like it. Love your neighbour like yourself. All the law and the prophets hang on these two commandments" (Mt. 22.37-40). Another time Jesus said that if one has faith and does not doubt one can even move mountains (Mt. 21.21-22). The episode of asking a drink of water from the Samaritan woman (John 4.9) shows that Jesus believed in the sisterhood and brotherhood of human beings and that he acted accordingly. The example he set is much more valuable than exhortation.

Teaching Methods used by the Buddha and Christ

The Kevaṭṭa Sutta of the Dīgha Nikāya enumerates three miraculous powers of the Buddha, namely, the miracle of performing supernatural feats (*iddhipāṭihāriya*), the miracle of thought reading (*ādesanāpāṭihāriya*), and the miracle of instruction (*anusāsanapāṭihāriya*).[38] Of these three what is valued most is the miracle of instruction or the extraordinary power of teaching. The first two are subservient to the last and as such they will be discussed under methods of instruction.

The Aṅguttara Nikāya elucidates five principles which a teacher should keep in mind when instructing his disciples.[39]

(1) He should arrange the subject matter in a logical sequence which gradually leads from simple to more difficult issues, from the known to the unknown.
(2) He should present the subject matter so that the main thesis is highlighted.
(3) He should have compassion towards his disciples.
(4) He should not expect any reward or material gain.

(5) He should present the subject matter in impersonal language without any reference to oneself or others.

In conformity with these principles of teaching the Buddha makes use of several methods or techniques for the elucidation of ideas. Most of the suttas are straightforward discourses, some are dialogues, a few are debates. Similes, anecdotes and even miracles are utilized at appropriate times to communicate ideas convincingly. All the teaching methods aim at helping the disciples to discover truths through personal experience. Discovery by oneself is most important to bring about transformation of attitude and character.

Buddhism recognizes three levels of understanding or knowledge, namely, book knowledge (*sutamayapaññā*), logical knowledge (*cintāmayapaññā*), and experiential knowledge (*bhāvanāmayapaññā*).[40] The first comprises the acceptance of truths on faith. When a six-year old child is taught that the earth is spherical, he accepts it on faith in the teacher, and his knowledge remains at information level. A fifteen-year old boy understands the same truth at an intellectual level based on logical inferences. That is the second level. An astronaut who sees the planet earth from outer space knows the same truth at experiential level. Similarly, all truths taught in Buddhism have to be ultimately realized at the experiential level through mental culture and equanimous awareness. All teaching methods have this self-realization as their ultimate aim.

The following paragraphs will be devoted to a brief discussion of the nature of discourses, debates, similes, anecdotes and miracles used in the service of education.

Discourses

Clarity of presentation is the most important feature in the discourses of the Buddha. He develops the ideas he wishes to communicate in a logical sequence, explaining details step by step utilizing the principle of leading the disciple from the known to the unknown. The graduated sermons generally start with simple virtues and lead up to more difficult concepts. The following is an example of the general order of ideas presented: the value of charity (*dānakathā*), the nobility of virtuous conduct (*sīlakathā*), the rewards thereof in the hereafter (*saggakathā*), the evil consequences, banality and impurity of sense pleasures (*kāmānaṁ ādinavaṁ okāraṁ saṅkilesaṁ*) and the benefits of renunciation (*nekkhamme ānisaṁsaṁ*).[41] Thus there is a gradual build-up from the known simple truths to the more sophisticated unknown areas of truth and virtue.

The Buddha had absolute clarity of thought, therefore he was in a position to present clear-cut ideas. He analyzed concepts into their constituent elements, labelled and numbered them so meticulously that the disciples had an orderly frame of reference for sorting out and connecting ideas, and for assimilating them easily and retaining them in memory without difficulty. For example, the human being is presented as a psycho-physical unit (*nāmarūpa*) which can be further analyzed into five aggregates of form (*rūpa*), feeling (*vedanā*), perception (*saññā*), volitional activities (*saṅkhārā*) and consciousness (*viññāṇa*). Each and every aggregate is again analyzed into its elements, paving the way for the emergence of their universal characteristics of impermanence (*anicca*), unsatisfactory nature (*dukkha*) and egolessness (*anattā*).

When a person comes for a discussion the Buddha would not straight away criticize his cherished views however objectionable they may be. Taking up the interlocutor's idea as the starting point, the Buddha would gradually lead the discussion to higher and higher levels until there dawns on the interlocutor step by step the triviality of the ideas he originally held and the nobility of the ideas presented by the Buddha.

The Kūṭadanta Sutta can be cited as a typical example of this method.[42] A brahmin named Kūṭadanta wished to know from the Buddha the advantages of offering a sacrifice as he intended to perform a great sacrifice. In order to elucidate the advantages, the Buddha narrates an ancient story the gist of which conveys the idea that a sacrifice which involves no killing, no cutting of trees, and no harassment to slaves is far better than the traditional sacrifice which involves all these. Giving alms is better than sacrificing, giving alms to the virtuous is still better, practising virtue is more commendable, and so forth. Thereby he leads the brahmin up to the idea of the attainment of Nibbāna, which is supreme and beyond which there is nothing better. Thus a man who had the intention of offering a bloody sacrifice by killing hundreds of animals was easily converted and never was a word of direct criticism uttered to attack his original view, which was steeped in the Vedic sacrificial tradition.

Many more instances of this nature could be cited, but the space of a short paper does not permit such detail. It is very important to remember that the Buddha refrained from criticizing other religious and philosophical views as far as possible, but if and when occasion demanded he was bold enough to call a spade a spade. As a general rule he preferred to expound the Dhamma which he himself discovered rather than point an accusing finger at other ideologies.

Debates

There are a few interesting instances when the Buddha was challenged to debates. The Cūḷasaccaka Sutta is a noteworthy example.[43] Here we see that the Buddha gets his opponent to clearly state his case at the very outset. Sometimes he would get his opponent to repeat the main point of his thesis thrice so that there is no doubt even in the minds of the members of the audience regarding his point of view.[44] Starting from that the Buddha would end the argument in such a way that the opponent ends up in a dilemma. Whether he says yes or no, he is vanquished in the debate. If he says yes he agrees with the Buddha, if he says no he contradicts himself. With crystal clear ideas and logical argument the Buddha was able to win over even the most redoubtable and arrogant debaters of his day.

Some debaters came to the Buddha with premeditated dilemmas. For example, Abhayarājakumāra was instructed by the Jaina Mahāvīra to ask the Buddha whether he would utter unpleasant words.[45] If the Buddha says no he should be reminded of the words he spoke to Devadatta that he would have to face dire consequences for his vicious deeds, and those were no pleasant words to Devadatta. But if he says yes, he should be asked what is the difference between him and an ordinary man. Thus the dilemma was prearranged. But when the question was put, the Buddha replied that no categorical answer could be given to that question, and the debater could not proceed further as he had not envisaged such a reply. There are times when the Buddha speaks unpleasant words out of compassion for the individual concerned. Intelligent men had the highest respect for the Buddha for the way he handled debaters, and such an appreciation is recorded in the Dhammacetiya Sutta.[46]

Similes

The simile is a much exploited teaching method in the Pali Canon. Experiential truths which cannot be communicated through descriptions or logical arguments can be clarified to a certain extent with the help of similes. Therefore it is a very effective teaching technique. A couple of examples would illustrate their efficacy. In the Aggivacchagotta Sutta[47] the question regarding the state of the arahant after death is raised: (a) Does the Tathāgata exist after death? (b) Does he not exist after death? (c) Does he exist and not exist after death? (d) Does he neither exist nor not exist after death? The Buddha has left these questions unanswered as it is neither possible nor useful to answer them. Why the Buddha adopts such an attitude is illustrated with a simile. When there is a fire burning we know that the fire is burning, and when it goes out we know that it has gone out. But if the question is asked in which direction did the fire go, east, south, west or north, it cannot be answered. Similar is the question of the state of the arahant after death. Thus the simile is an eloquent device to convey some idea regarding that which cannot be expressed in words.

The simile is also an impressive means of communicating abstruse ideas. The human personality is constituted with the five aggregates of grasping. The five are so interconnected and interlaced with one another that it is just not possible to physically set them apart. Just as when five oils are mixed up in one vessel, the different kinds of oils cannot be separated, so intermixed are the five aggregates.[48]

Long exhortations could sometimes be dispensed with by the employment of a simile. It kindles the imagination and paves the way for self-discovery. For instance, the layperson is admonished to accumulate wealth just as the bee collects pollen from the flowers.[49] This is a thought-provoking terse simile, the rich implications of which could be expanded into a number of pages. Such is the use of similes and they are abundantly employed in the Pali Canon.

Parables

The parable is closely akin to the simile, so much so that sometimes the one can pass for the other. But anecdotes which can be strictly called parables are less frequently employed in the Pali Canon. However, if some of the Jātaka stories can be classified as parables, then it can be said that the parable is extensively used in Buddhist literature as a method of instruction. It appears that the identification of characters at the end (*samodhāna*) prevents Jātaka stories from being classified as parables.

From the Canon the Pāyāsirājañña Sutta can be cited as a good example where a number of parables are used to illustrate ideas.[50] Pāyāsi was a die-hard materialist who believed that there is no survival after death. He explained to the monk Kumārakassapa that he came to this conclusion after conducting some experiments with convicted prisoners. He boiled them in carefully sealed vessels and when he was fairly certain that the victims were dead, he slowly opened the vessel to see the soul escaping. But he never saw a soul. After a series of such gruesome experiments he came to the firm conclusion that the individual does not survive after death. Kumārakassapa explained the inappropriate nature of his experiments with the help of a parable. A conch blower went to a remote village and blew his conch shell thrice. Villagers came rushing and inquired from where that lovely sound came. The man showed them that conch shell. Then they placed it in different positions, shook it hard, and beat it with sticks in their attempt to make it sound, but no sound came. The conch blower thought how foolish these villages are to look for the sound of the conch shell in such a stupid manner.

Stories

Stories are a beautiful teaching device utilized for illustrating doctrinal points. They enliven serious doctrinal discussions by lending a simple literary charm while at the same time making difficult concepts intelligible. The Mahāsudassana Sutta is a long story describing the splendour of King Mahāsudassana's kingdom.[51] At the end of the story the universal truth of impermanence (*anicca*) is highlighted as even such a magnificent kingdom has perished in course of time. The *Vimānavatthu* and *Petavatthu* contain ample stories, both long and short, to elucidate the theory of kamma and rebirth. The Jātakas are another beautiful collection of stories which on the whole illustrate the fact that deeds repeatedly performed have a cumulative effect on character not only in one lifetime, but over repeated births. That is how the persistent performance of virtuous action ultimately brings about enlightenment. Stories are very effective means of educating children and also those who are intellectually immature. Their efficacy as a medium of teaching moral values even to mature adults cannot be underestimated.

Special Techniques for Self-Realization

Usual methods of Buddhist meditation such as *ānāpānasati*, *asubhabhāvanā* and *vedanānupassanā*—awareness of respiration, bodily impurity and feelings, respectively—generally lead to self-realization or experiential knowledge (*bhāvanāmayapaññā*), which was mentioned in the early part of this essay. But there are exceptional circumstances when they do not yield rapid results, and at a time like that it is only a Buddha who can give a suitable topic of meditation.

The case of Cūḷapanthaka is an excellent example.[52] Cūḷapanthaka was so dull-witted that he could not memorize even a single stanza over a period of some months. His teacher, who happened to be his brother, asked him to leave the Order as no useful purpose could be served by such a stupid person remaining as a monk. Sadly Cūḷapanthaka was preparing to leave when the Buddha discovered him. The Buddha gave him a fresh piece of white cloth and asked him to sit in the sun stroking the piece of cloth while repeating the words "removing dust, removing dust" (*rajoharaṇaṁ rajoharaṇaṁ*). Cūḷapanthaka started this exercise and when the sun rose high he began perspiring profusely. He noticed that the clean white cloth which he was stroking had become dirty and this made him become aware of the impure nature of the body. This train of thought gradually became deeper and deeper, and before noon he realized the true nature of all phenomena and became an arahant.

Another similar episode is related in the Titthajātaka[53] where a pupil of Sāriputta could not make any progress for four months with the meditation topic of bodily impurity. At last Sāriputta took him to the Buddha who discovered that bodily impurity was not a suitable topic for him as he had been a goldsmith in a number of previous births. As he was used to working with bright objects he needed a beautiful topic of meditation. The Buddha advised him to meditate on a full-blown lotus in the beautiful setting of a pond. He began the exercise and as time went on the lotus started fading, as naturally it would. This drove the truth of impermanence home so thoroughly that by the same evening he became an arahant.

The Buddha has the unique teaching ability of prescribing the most suitable meditation topic for different individuals as he has insight into their character traits and mental propensities. It is therefore not without absolutely valid reason that he is called the teacher of gods and men (*satthā devamanussānaṁ*), and the supreme guide of tameable men (*anuttaro purisadammasārathi*).

The grief-stricken mother Kisā Gotamī came to the Buddha hugging her dead child, imploring the Buddha to cure him.[54] The Buddha asked her to bring some mustard seeds from a house where no death has occurred. Mustard was famous for its medicinal properties and Kisā Gotamī's hopes rose high. With fresh courage she went from house to house, but although she could get plenty of mustard seeds, she could get none from a house where no one had died. As she went on, gradually it dawned on her that death is not her individual woe, that it is a universal fact. Her grief thinned, she disposed of the child's body, and then went back to the Buddha and became a nun. Disciplining herself according to the Master's advice, before long she became an arahant.

Thus the teaching methods employed by the Buddha are most ingenious, and at times intriguing, and the fact remains that they have been very effective for the development of insight and transformation of character.

Miracles in the Service of Instruction

Though the ability to perform miracles is one of the six supernormal knowledges (*abhiññā*), it is not a faculty indispensable for the attainment of arahantship. Of the six, it is the one of least importance. The Buddha discouraged their performance even though some of his disciples had achieved great miraculous powers. It is an extra ability which develops when one practises meditation to discipline the mind.

Once a layman hoisted a sandalwood bowl on the top of a high pole and challenged any holy person to rise up and take it. Many mendicants belonging to other religious sects tried and failed. An arahant named Piṇḍolabhāradvāja rose into the air through his miraculous power and took the bowl, and received much acclaim from on-looking laymen. The Buddha rebuked him in strong words for using his abilities for an unworthy end, and had the bowl ground into sandal-paste and distributed among the monks.[55] So unrelenting was the Buddha's attitude to the cheap display of miracles.

At times the Buddha made use of his miraculous powers as an effective method of teaching the Dhamma. The episode of the conversion of Queen Khemā is a noteworthy example.[56] Khemā was exceedingly beautiful and was proud of her beauty. She disliked going to see the Buddha as she had heard that the Buddha speaks ill of beauty. One day the king coerced her and she paid a visit to the Buddha. The Buddha created, before her eyes, the figure of a beautiful young girl fanning him. Khemā was surprised and pleased to see such a beauty. All her attention was focussed on this beautiful girl, and while she still continued gazing, gradually the beauty started passing through the phases of middle age and old age. At last as a decrepit old woman she slumped to the ground and died. Khemā was convinced of the evanescent nature of beauty and her intoxication with her own beauty subsided. She became a nun, worked diligently and soon realized arahantship.

The story of Nanda is another interesting example.[57] Nanda was dissatisfied with his life as a monk and constantly thought of the girl he was betrothed to. He sought the Buddha's permission to disrobe. The Buddha took him to heaven with his miraculous powers and showed him beautiful celestial nymphs. But on the way to heaven he made it a point to draw Nanda's attention to an old she-monkey sitting on a burnt tree stump. Nanda was fascinated with the celestial nymphs, and when the Buddha asked what he thought of his lady love, he said that compared to these nymphs she is like the she-monkey whom they saw on the wayside. The Buddha promised that Nanda would obtain these celestial nymphs if only he set his mind on meditation. He meditated diligently and as he progressed he became disinterested in sense pleasures and ultimately became an arahant. Enjoying great peace of mind he came to the Buddha with gratitude and released the Buddha from the promise he made about gaining the celestial nymphs.

Thus the Buddha appreciated only the instrumental value of miraculous powers, as an effective aid to spiritual education, to be used at appropriate times. He did not rely on them as an infallible convincing instrument of conversion. The ability to perform miracles could be gained through the type of magic called Gandhārī as well,[58] and not necessarily through mental culture. Therefore the Buddha did not see any intrinsic spiritual value in miracles. In fact miraculous powers could spell one's downfall if one was not spiritually motivated and emotionally mature. The glaring example is Devadatta, who came to utter ruin through the development of miraculous powers and the gain and honour which came to him in their wake.[59]

Seeking the Needy and the Worthy

The Buddha was an indefatigable teacher and he did not wait until disciples came to him. Often he went walking many miles on foot, seeking those who could benefit from his teachings, extending a helping hand to the needy. Sunīta was a low caste scavenger despised and cornered by society. The Buddha observed the spark of spiritual maturity shining through him and walked up to him. Thus Sunîta had the opportunity of joining the community of monks and realizing the spiritual goal.[60] Angulimāla was a learned young man who had become a highway robber and a murderer due to wicked circumstances. The Buddha approached him out of compassion and changed his ignoble character into that of a worthy saint.[61] Suppabuddha was a leper who strayed into the congregation where the Buddha was preaching, thinking that food was being distributed there. The Buddha preached having his understanding capacity particularly in mind and he became a stream-enterer.[62] Maṭṭa-kuṇḍali the miser's son lay on his death-bed as his father was too stingy to spend on his medicine. The Buddha approached him and he was overjoyed to see the serene countenance of the Buddha radiant with wisdom and compassion. He was able to breathe his last in great joy and was reborn a deity.[63]

The Buddha devoted his entire life of forty-five years after the attainment of enlightenment for the purpose of preaching out of compassion for the suffering masses. Even on his death-bed shortly before his final passing away he was not without a pupil. He instructed a mendicant named Subhadda and led him on the spiritual path. Thus until the very last he rendered spiritual service to all those who came in contact with him and each one benefited according to his or her capacity for understanding and his or her moral stature.

Teaching Methods of Jesus Christ

Though the words "teaching" and "preaching" occur practically on all the pages of the Gospels we can glean very little material from the Bible on the role of Jesus Christ as teacher and his teaching techniques. In a number of places in the New Testament it is said that Jesus went from place to place teaching and preaching, but the Bible does not record the contents of his teachings in these itineraries. The reason perhaps is that his role as teacher is subservient to that of saviour.

The Sermon on the Mount alone could be strictly called a discourse. There he exhorts people to be righteous and compassionate, and to lead simple lives without being overly anxious about worldly concerns such as food, clothing and shelter. It is a clear and straight-forward exhortation inspired by wisdom and compassion. People were amazed at the authority and spontaneity with which he spoke, and the Christian tradition explains that he had divine authority to preach. But someone outside the theistic tradition could interpret his convincing authority and spontaneity to have sprung from the fact that he preached what he practised. He exhorted people to have faith, and he displayed by his behaviour that he himself had faith in God. He admonished people on the importance of forgiveness and he forgave even those who tortured him. He believed in the brotherhood of man and he showed it by going into the homes of the despised and having meals with them. Thus his teaching was effective because he practised what he preached.

The parable is an important teaching technique which Jesus employed. He drew his material from daily experiences of family life, from fields, plants, fishing gear, etc. The parable allows the listener to draw his conclusions regarding the point the teacher wishes to illustrate. In most of the parables Jesus tries to explain some aspect or other of the kingdom of heaven. Jesus says: The kingdom of heaven is like a farmer who sowed good seeds in his field. But while everyone was sleeping an enemy came and sowed weeds among the wheat and went away. When the wheat sprouted and formed heads, then the weeds also appeared.

The weeds were allowed to grow along with the wheat lest the roots of the wheat get loosened if the weeds are pulled. At harvest time the weeds were collected and burnt, and the wheat was taken to the barn (Mt.13.24-30). The moral is that the good people will be taken care of by God while the bad will be consigned to hell fires.

The parable of the net is another typical example. It says: The kingdom of heaven is like a net that was let down into the lake and caught all kinds of fish. When it was full, the fisherman pulled it up on the shore. Then they sat down and collected the good fish in baskets, but threw the bad away. This is how it will be at the end of the age. The angels will come and separate the wicked from the righteous and throw them into the fiery furnace, where there will be weeping and gnashing of teeth (Mt.13.47-50).

Thus to explain truths which lay beyond the ambit of logic Jesus made use of parables. His central message was the kingdom of God, or the kingdom of heaven, as it is sometimes called. With parables he seems to have explained that the kingdom of God is within each and every human being and that at the time of death those who have led righteous lives will be rewarded while those who have not will be punished.

There is evidence to show that Jesus Christ also employed subtle methods to evaluate current social traditions. Once when he was seated teaching a large gathering of followers the Pharisees brought him a woman caught in adultery (John 8). According to the law of Moses such women should be stoned and they asked Jesus what should be done. Jesus became pensive and without looking at the crowd he said: "If any one of you is without sin, let him be the first to throw a stone at her." Those who heard this began to go away one at a time until at last Jesus was left alone with the woman still standing there. Thus in a most inoffensive way Jesus made the people realize the futility of some socially accepted customs. In a periphrastic way he also showed the importance of self-assessment.

Miracles form an integral part of the Gospel tradition. It is said that they can no more be eliminated from the records than a watermark can be removed from a sheet of paper.[64] They are given pride of place in Christianity and are called the mighty works. Jesus himself regarded them as great work, for when John the Baptist sent his disciples to find out if Jesus is the messiah, Jesus replied: "Go back and report to John what you hear and see: The blind receive sight, the lame walk, those who have leprosy are cured, the deaf hear, the dead are raised, and the good news is preached to the poor" (Mt.11.4-5). Jesus may not have exploited his miraculous powers just to win the faith of the people, but because he believed them to be an important gift and authority given by God. They are traditionally believed to be proof of the heavenly origin of Jesus and his divine sonship of God.

Modern scholarship regards miracles as God's sovereign grace and forgiveness operative in Christ.[65] Jesus is said to speak to the Father on behalf of the sinners. Jesus is the righteous one. He is the atoning sacrifice for the sins of all, for the sins of the whole world (1 John 2.1-2). Therefore miracles had a special relevance in the context of Christianity, as they helped to evoke faith in the beholders. Here we are reminded of a conversation between Jesus Christ, Thomas and Philip as recorded in John 14.5-12.

> Thomas said to him: "Lord, we don't know where you are going, so how can we know the way?"
>
> Jesus answered: "I am the way and the truth and the life. No one comes to the Father except through me. If you really know me, you would know my Fa-

> ther as well. From now on, you do know him and have seen him."
>
> Philip said: "Lord, show us the Father and that will be enough for us."
>
> Jesus answered: "Don't you know me, Philip, even after I have been among you such a long time? Anyone who has seen me has seen the Father. How can you say, 'Show us the Father?' Don't you believe that I am in the Father and that the Father is in me? The words I say to you are not just my own. Rather it is the Father, living in me, who is doing his work. Believe me when I say that I am in the Father and the Father is in me: or at least believe on the evidence of the miracles themselves."

As can be seen from the above quotation faith is an important virtue in Christianity. One has to believe that Jesus Christ is the son of God and that salvation can come only through him. There is no way of proving or knowing this, one has to simply believe it through an act of faith. In this context the miracle plays an important role. A miracle is an extraordinary, supernatural event, and when it does happen it is to be taken as good proof of supernatural intervention. Therefore the miracle was extensively used as a means of educating the people to believe in the message of Jesus Christ.

Thus it is possible to maintain that the parable and the miracle are the most important methods of teaching employed by Jesus Christ.

Conclusion

When we compare the Pali Canon with the New Testament of the Bible we cannot help but notice that the former is an extensive storehouse of literature while the latter is only a single volume. The Buddha's ministry lasted forty-five years whereas Jesus Christ had a short ministry of about three years. Perhaps the very discrepancy in the length of the ministry is responsible for the difference in the volume of scripture. On the other hand, the functions of the two spiritual leaders also differed from each other. The Buddha declared truths which he himself discovered with his intuitive wisdom. He emphatically affirmed that the truths he preaches have not been heard from another source, but he understood them by himself, saw them himself and knew them personally.[66] In contrast, Jesus Christ is emphatic in maintaining that he is the spokesman of God. He says: "My teaching is not my own. It comes from him who sent me" (John 7.16). He exhorts his disciples too not to worry about what to say in case they are arrested, and assures them saying: "At that time you will be given what to say, for it will not be you speaking, but the spirit of your Father speaking through you" (Mt.10.19-20).

The Buddha was essentially a teacher whereas Jesus Christ was a saviour. A modern scholar succinctly describes Jesus Christ's role when he says: it is not the teaching of Christ that saves, but the Christ who teaches.[67] The very opposite could be said of the Buddha. Therefore there is a fundamenal difference between the two spiritual leaders. According to the very function of the Buddha there should be extensive literature expounding all aspects of the Dhamma so that disciples could learn and put it into practice to achieve the same liberation that the Buddha achieved for himself. Dearth of literature is no problem for Christianity, for if one has absolute faith in Jesus Christ and if one leads a reasonably righteous life, that is sufficient for salvation. There is hardly any mention of mental culture in the Bible.

The attainment of liberation essentially takes place

within the lifetime of a person according to Buddhism, but salvation according to Christianity can be achieved only after death. Development of wisdom and compassion at a profound level in this very life is essential for liberation according to the former, but absolute faith is the necessary condition for salvation according to the latter.

These differences in the soteriology of the two religions are reflected in the role of the two spiritual leaders as teachers. The Buddha had to make use of effective methods of teaching to make his disciples understand the Dhamma so that each one could make a Dhamma-raft for himself for the purpose of crossing over from the misery of *saṁsāric* existence to the bliss of Nibbāna. Jesus Christ had to utilize mainly faith-evoking devices such as miracles as it is through faith in him that his disciples could achieve salvation. Jesus himself says: "Unless you people see miraculous signs and wonders you will never believe" (John 4.48).

NOTES

All Pali books referred to are editions of the Pali Text Society, England. Roman figures denote volume numbers and Arabic figures denote page numbers.

ABBREVIATIONS

A	Aṅguttara Nikāya
D	Dîgha Nikāya
Dhp	Dhammapada
DhpA	Dhammapada Aṭṭhakathā
J	Jātaka Aṭṭhakathā
M	Majjhima Nikāya
S	Saṁyutta Nikāya
Thig	Therîgāthā
ThigA	Therîgāthā Aṭṭhakathā
Ud	Udāna
Vin	Vinaya Piṭaka

1. D.I,87, 111, 127, etc.
2. Dhp.v.276.
3. *Encyclopaedia of Religion and Ethics*, s.v. Jesus Christ.
4. Ibid.
5. *The Concise Encyclopedia of Living Faiths*, ed. R.C. Zaehner, 1959, p.52.
6. Vin.I,10; S.II,10. *Pubbe ananussutesu dhammesu cakkhuṁ udapādi.*
7. M.I,71.
8. Visuddhimagga I,318. *Paradukkhe sati sādhūnaṁ hadayakampanaṁ karoti.*

9. Suttanipāta Aṭṭhakathā 128. *Ahita-dukkhāpanaya-kāmatā karuṇā.*
10. Ibid. *Hita-sukhūpanaya-kāmatā mettā.*
11. Dīghanikāya Aṭṭhakathā Ṭīkā I,3. *Karuṇā-nidānā hi sabbe pi buddhaguṇā.*
12. Ibid. I,9.
13. Paṭisambhidāmagga I,126; DhpA.I,26, 367.
14. M.I,129.
15. Dhp.vv. 129-30. *Attānaṁ upamaṁ katvā na haneyya na ghātaye.*
16. M.I,129.
17. S.V,438.
18. D.II,100.
19. D.I,187-89.
20. S.IV,272, etc.
21. Dhp.v.19-20, 64-65.
22. M.I,118; S.IV,373; A.IV,139.
23. M.I,134.
24. M.I,234, 260.
25. James S. Stewart, *The Life and Teaching of Jesus Christ.* London: SCM Press, 1958, pp.48-55.
26. Vin.I,21.
27. A.IV, 202.
28. Vin.I,182.
29. DhpA.I,319-20.
30. D.II,224.
31. M.I,317-20.
32. M.I,444.
33. M.I,457.
34. DhpA.III,417-21.
35. M.I,395.
36. M.III,117-18.
37. S.III,120.
38. D.I,212.

39. A.III,184.
40. D.III,219.
41. Vin.I,15.
42. D.I,127-49.
43. M.I,227-37.
44. M.I,372.
45. M.I,392.
46. M.II,122-23.
47. M.I,487.
48. Majjhimanikāya Aṭṭhakathā II,344-45.
49. D.II,188.
50. D.II,337-38.
51. D.II,169-99.
52. DhpA.I,244-47.
53. J.I,182-83.
54. ThigA.174.
55. Vin.II,110-12.
56. ThigA.128.
57. Ud.21-23.
58. D.I,213.
59. Vin.II,183; S.II,241.
60. Theragāthā, vv. 620-631.
61. M.II,97-100.
62. Ud.48-50.
63. DhpA.I,27.
64. A.M. Hunter, *The Work and Words of Jesus*, Madras 1969, p.59.
65. Ibid., pp.60-61.
66. M.III,186. *Nāññassa samaṇassa vā brāhmaṇassa vā sutvā vadāmi. Api ca yad eva me sāmañ ñātaṁ sāmaṁ diṭṭhaṁ sāmaṁ viditaṁ, tam ev' ahaṁ vadāmi.*
67. Stewart, *The Life and Teaching of Jesus Christ*, p.67.

ABOUT THE AUTHOR

Lily de Silva is Professor of Pali and Buddhist Studies at the University of Peradeniya in Sri Lanka. A regular contributor to Buddhist scholarly and popular journals, she is also the editor of the subcommentary to the Digha Nikāya, published by the Pali Text Society of London. Her previous BPS publications are *One Foot in the World* (Wheel No.337/338), *The Self-Made Private Prison* (Bodhi Leaves No.120), and *Radical Therapy* (Bodhi Leaves No.123).

Also from BPS

AN ANALYSIS OF THE PALI CANON

Edited by Russell Webb

The Pali Canon is our oldest source for the original teachings of the historical Buddha. To guide the student through this vast compilation of texts the unsurpassed guide for decades has been *An Analysis of the Pali Canon.* The book contains a textual analysis of the canon, an index to its principal parts, and a full bibliography of translations and scholarly studies.

Softback: 112 pages — 124 mm x 182 mm
U.S.$4.50; £.3.00: SL Rs.90 — Order No. WH 217/220

KAMMA AND ITS FRUIT

Edited by Nyanaponika Thera

Kamma, or karma, is the Buddhist conception of willed action as a force which shapes and transforms human destiny. In this book five practising Buddhists offer their reflections on the significance of kamma and its relations to ethics, spiritual practice, and philosophical understanding.

Softback: 128 pages — 124 mm x 182 mm
U.S. $4.50; £ 3.00; SL Rs.90 — Order No. WH 221/224

THE BUDDHIST PUBLICATION SOCIETY